HAIKU YOUR PARENT LEFT YOU TO

Poems by Cindy Khoo
Art by Maya Chungbin

ISBN: 9798862386189 (paperback)

CONTENTS

DEDICATION

For mom. You created me, broke me,
and inspired me to create. This book is because
of you and in spite of you.

ACKNOLWEDGEMENTS

For Em, who believes in me even when I don't. She's the ultimate hype woman who sees the boss that she is in others, dedicating her time to creating spaces for writers to flourish and set audacious goals. Thank you for creating Author Lab and telling me to take the poems and illustrations analog! Big hugs to our group as well! Your energy fueled my pages and I know you're all lighting up the literary world in your own unique ways.

For Courtney, author, talent, friend, and free spirit. I'd been dragging my nuts on this book for years, which is not like me at all. I'm a Virgo. We get things done. You might not remember this, but on an uncharacteristically rainy LA night we were talking books and when I started giving reasons (ahem, excuses) over why this wasn't getting done, you asked me in your lovely, gentle, curious, nurturing way: "what resistance do you have with writing this book?" It was all I needed to get my arse in gear, and well here we are.

For Nat, who I can only describe as the best trip if acid were a person. You are the total package and a literary POWERHOUSE. Thank you for gassing me up, making me laugh, being the most, and all you've done for me, women, and people of color. You are truly one of a kind and I guarantee I would not be laying poems to page if you hadn't reached out to me years ago. At the time, it seemed random but now that I am blessed to know you, I see it is as fate.

Thank you to Sarah and Counter Claim magazine for publishing my work and for being such an inspiration. You are a true renaissance woman and I am in awe of your commitment to creativity and community.

X's and O's to my writing groups - The Artists Way and the Monday night Shut Up & Write crew. Thank you for keeping me accountable! Your energy has been pivotal especially in the final stages of this book.

Maya, I am in awe of your talent and the life your illustrations brought to this book. Fresh, thoughtful, and cool, I could not have asked for a better collaborator.

And lastly, thank you to my parents. The Universe may have given me the words, but you gave me the experience. Both are gifts. I know that now.

INTRODUCTION

I was a year old.
Unreliability
was my first lesson.

My mother left my father when I was a year old. Their marriage was failing long before I arrived. He was a narcissist and she was conflict avoidant. I learned those words in therapy. She asked him to go to therapy once. He made her regret it.

At no point in my childhood did it occur to me that she'd also left me too. My dad was fragile, his pain bigger than anyone else's.

And so I became small.

I acted just fine
when I wasn't, to survive.
To make you feel big.

My dad told me I was fine. That my mom's absence didn't bother me. I believed him and agreed. Not because it was true, but because I had to. Because he needed to feel like a good parent. A big man. That was important to him.

But how could it not bother me? How could I have lived in her stomach, heard her voice, felt her breath, her every movement and not have felt anything when she left? My dad's an idiot.

I was occupied
with life, appearing afloat
but inside I drowned,

choked on salty tears
spoon fed by my dad because
he was all I had.

For a while, I was OK. I really was by anyone's standards. College. Job. Friends. Boyfriends. But I hated my mother. Part of it was the half-truths my dad told me. He told me she left because she didn't want to be a mother. It wasn't true, but how was I to know that? She never told him either, so how was he to know that? He told his own narratives with him cast as the hero and her as the villain. Those became my bedtime stories.

He told his story, and now I tell mine.

I started out writing this book for myself because I was tired of pretending to be fine. Pretending to my dad, pretending to the world, and pretending to myself. Even pretending in therapy! "My mom did her best. I have empathy and compassion for her, and so I forgive her. No, I'm not mad. No, I'm not bitter." HAH!

With that initial intention of self-expression, I was writing poetry. A good amount too. But I would inevitably hit a wall. There were bursts and then slumps of blank pages. I would emotionally empty myself and then have nothing for months. It wasn't until I joined an Author Lab where our eclectic and straight shooting leader asked us:

"Who needs to read this book?"

It was in that thought exercise that I realized I needed to write this book for all others who had been abandoned by their parent(s). I knew I wasn't the only one. Growing up, how I wished someone heard me. How I wished I had the permission to be heard.

No one will ever truly know what it is like having a parent abandon you unless you've lived through that special void. You may share parts of your story with well-meaning friends, only to have their eyes glaze over, not knowing what to say, eventually making you feel dismissed. You'll stop sharing because you were left once already, and you're really not in the mood to have your story abandoned too. But here's the thing -

They're not going to get it because they're not supposed to. No one is supposed to know what it is like to be left by their mother or father. YOU were not supposed to know.

My hope with this book is that through these words, your

Pain
Anxiety
Panic
Confusion
Resilience
Independence

...all that your parent(s) took away, and all that they left you with are understood. I want you to feel less alone because when it really mattered, YOU were left alone.

With Love and Empathy

Cindy Khoo

What do you do when
The one person who's supposed
to stay with you, leaves?

1

IF ONLY

If only the good
in me outweighed the bad then
maybe you would stay.

LOVE, MOM

"She was elegant.
Sophisticated, so I
knew it wasn't you."

The worst parts of me
are the reasons you left and
why I hate myself.

"You look better when
you don't smile." A loving note,
from a mother to

her daughter. I cried.
I was angry. I also
stopped smiling that day.

Once you said my hair
was ugly. For years I thought
maybe that was why.

LOVE, ME

One day I'll wake up
and I will look lovingly
in the mirror at

My messy hair and
giant front teeth, soft belly,
and I will love her

Unconditionally.

And you? You'll be a
Mother who said horrible
things, who loved herself

Conditionally.

2

ANXIETY

Panicked and alone,
I looked for you, looked for help,
grasping at nothing.

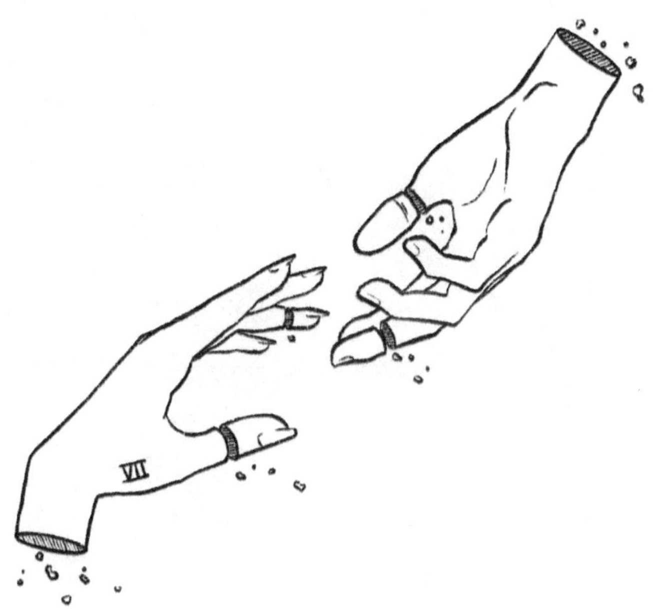

IRRECONCILABLE DIFFERENCES

"Let's have a baby!"
Hate to spoil the ending but,
it never works out.

For you, I was a
Solution to your marriage.
For me, you were mom.

When aftershocks of
divorce and their cracked marriage
were never your fault.

EVERYONE AROUND ME

Before I was born
I came with a goal, which was
to solve the problems

of everyone around me.

I grew purposeful,
fulfilling your every need,
clueless to my own.

II

PILLS

Maybe I'll know calm.
Life, carefree. Maybe some day
I won't need these pills.

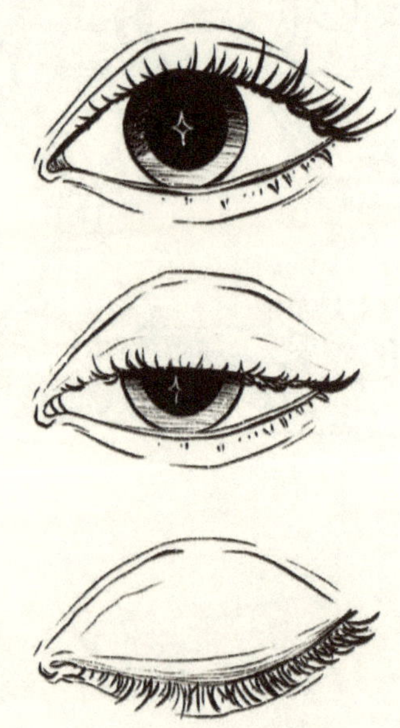

LACY PARK

Once, around the park
Mothers pushing their strollers,
you saw them and said

"I don't see that for you."

Now I carry your
careless prediction wishing
someone told you that.

MOTHERING

Is it mothering
that gives me dread? Or is it
mothering like you?

CONSTANTLY

I'm good at searching
for answers because often
I find them, but still

I search

because I don't know
the feeling of outstretched hands
filled. Met. And so I

let things go constantly.

3

IMPERMANENCE

Always ready to
let you go. Never prepared
to be without you.

What will I do with
your sincerity? Run? Or...
could I be happy?

Well I'd be lying
if I said it were all bad.
I've grown talented

                                        at saying goodbye.
                                 Master of impermanence.
                                    I'm a goddamn monk.

I don't miss people
because nothing compares to
the day you walked out.

He called me callous
for moving on. I've just had
a lot of practice.

Be without you for
a month? An eternity?
All the same to me.

You're gone but somehow
the thought of you soothes me more
than when you were here.

SHATTERED

It's hard to explain
why a broken mug hurts more
than a broken heart.

But I'll try.

It's just that people
leave, and can't be relied on.
But that mug held me

until it broke.

That's longer than you
were capable of. And now
that my mug is gone,

I am shattered.

4

RESILIENCE

It still bothers me
when you look at my walls and
say that they're ugly.

Then I'm reminded
of who the f*ck I am and
who the f*ck you are.

You,

who apologized
for leaving only after
saying I look fat.

You,

who told her daughter
it would have been easier
if she were not born.

You,

who does not say please,
and that my relationships
were a waste of time.

You,

unintentional
or not, who hurt me without
consideration.

So when you judge my
paint choices, I remember
that this is nothing.

That you've broken me
but I rebuilt and survived
it all. I survived

You.

The last petal fell.
"How sad," I thought. But the roots...
Those, I did not see.

BOTTOMLESS

The void you left is
bottomless and I will spend
a lifetime counting

syllables and days
waiting for you to show up,
for it to make sense.

But it never will.
And you never will. And all
I'll be left with is

poetry.

I WANTED YOU THERE

I wanted you there.
I wanted you to love me.
And so I became

desperate

for all the things you
could not give: support, love, pride.
And so I became

disappointed,

hurt and unaware
of your inabilities
and limitations.

You couldn't see me.
Maybe you didn't want to
because I remind

you of what you left,
where you should've been, and had
no hand in raising.

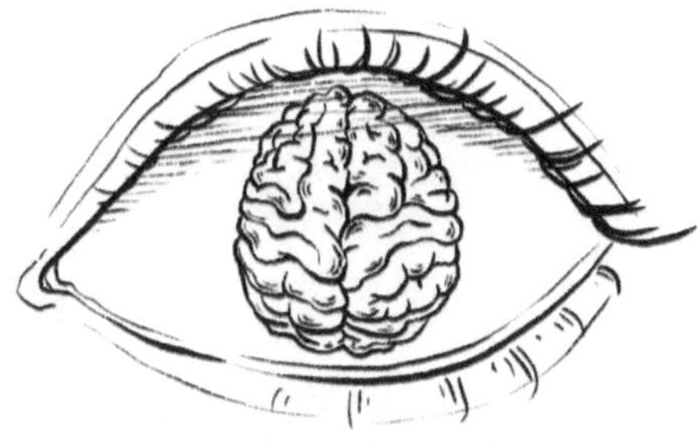

Your list of critiques
long and still counting. At least
you were creative.

Oh wait, that's me (;

NUMBER

GUIDE

*On a a few of the illustrations, you'll notice a Roman
numeral. They are related to numbers referenced in
numerology, tarot, and Angel numbers.*

IX

The number 9 symbolizes completion, but not
necessarily an ending. Rather, this number references
the cyclical nature of life. When one chapter ends,
another begins. Painful patterns repeat for the sake of
teaching lessons. We are hurt time and time again by
someone who criticizes us, who cannot love us, so that
one day, we learn to love ourselves.

VII

Seeing the number 7 points to the presence of angels
and spiritual guides during times when you feel
especially alone. Invisible protective forces see your
isolation and are there to carry you when you've been
abandoned. It's a number full of hope and marks the
beginning of budding of intuition, wisdom, and positive
influence. This number acknowledges the uncertainty
you are going through and lets you know that the
Universe has your back. It says, "I understand how they
left you. I understand what you've gone through. You
will grow up strong because of it. And for the times
when you are not, I am here." When you've been
abandoned by a parent, you may feel as if you are living
in a broken home. In time, you will wake up to the
realization that your home is complete because you are
complete, and you are your home.

II

The 2 of Cups card in tarot represents what can happen
when two entities come together. In an ideal world,
combined forces create a stronger bond, a sturdy
foundation with which to elevate. Many times though,
unhealthy connections are forged resulting in
codependency, toxic relationships, and pain for
everyone involved. The number 2 is a reminder to take a
look at who you are surrounding yourself with. Evaluate
those connections. Notice how empty or full your cup
feels after you spend time with people. If you find
yourself constantly drained, it may be time to
downgrade the amount of time and energy you spend
with certain people.

IV

The shadow planet, Rahu, positioned at the north node
of the moon is associated with the number 4. This is an
incredibly powerful number steeped in independence,
confidence, leadership, and general don't-give-a-
fuckery. It is the flip side of knowing that everything in
life is impermanent. It leads to a callousness in knowing
that since nothing lasts forever, what is the use of
making meaningful connections? It causes us to say
goodbye too early, to stop trying, not compromise, and
turn away in times when we have the opportunity to
turn to each other. We cut ourselves and our capacity
for love, connection, and intimacy short because we can
do it all on our own. We know this because there was so
much we had to do on our own. If you were abandoned

by a parent, figuring things out by yourself was a
necessity. There was no one around to teach you about
the beauty and discomfort of relationships. You learned
that when things get hard, the best thing to do is leave.
Those left behind will figure it out on their own. This
was your life. Have grace for yourself when you want to
cut and run. You were never taught to stay.

VIII

The number 8 is a stand-in for the infinity symbol ∞
turned on its side. It signifies eternity and regeneration.
Even when we have experienced what feels like a death
in the physical realm, this gives way to new thoughts,
qualities, and in some cases a new form. With
abandonment by a parent, it's a death of your innocence
and trust that gives way to an independence and
resourcefulness far beyond your years. This is not to
minimize the pain. I didn't say grief wouldn't hurt, only
that it will ignite other ways of existing. This number
also embodies the everlasting, constant nature of
energy. According to physics, energy cannot be created
or destroyed, only transformed. Our bodies are made
up of matter and energy. There is roughly 20 watts of
energy coursing through your body at any given
moment - enough to power a lightbulb. [2]Once your
physical form leaves the 3D world, those atoms and
energy are broken down and distributed into the world
as your "light," so you continue to exist only in a less
organized and compact way than when you inhabited
your body.

END NOTES

1. Preston, Lina Elisabeth, Rahu in Vedic Astrology. Northernlightsvedic.com. November 2022
2. Trosper, Jamie. *The Physics of Death.* Futurism.com. August 2019.

COMING

SOON

HAIKU TO HANDLE A NARCISSIST TO

Poems by Cindy Khoo

Heroes and villains.
There was she who left, and him
who stayed and broke me.

Cindy Khoo is the creator of My Emotional Armor
(MEA), a podcast dedicated to the adult survivors of
covert narcissistic parents. She uses her own experience
to humbly offer listeners the validation they've looked
for and gone too long without. The scars from this form
of abuse show up as frustration, anxiety, inauthenticity,
and lack of self trust.

MEA is a safe space for "robot warriors,"
a place to heal and be heard.

Email
myemotionalarmor@gmail.com

Listen
iTunes / Spotify / YouTube

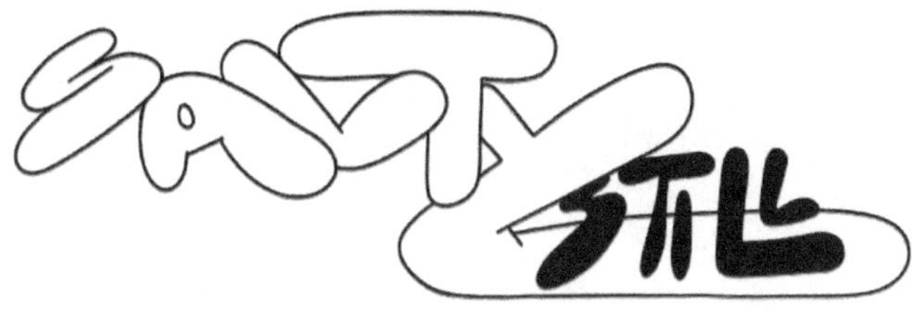

A freelance illustrator and brand designer based in Honolulu, Hawai'i, Maya came from humble beginnings, finding her start on Fiverr after making an account and tossing up some work just to see what it was about. She was thrown to the gig work wolves in 2020 after the pandemic shutdown and her little art fling suddenly became a full on design affair.

Maya's style hinges on making the weird and wonky look manicured. She's worked closely with 1000+ clients to bring design and illustration dreams and nightmares to life.

Website
saltystill.com

Instagram
@salty_still